CliffsNotes™

Woolf's
Mrs. Dalloway

By Gary Carey, M.A.

University of Colorado

▌ THIS BOOK

- ■ Life and Background
- ■ List of Characters
- ■ Critical Commentary
- ■ Character Analyses
- ■ Review Questions
- ■ Bibliography
- ■ Find additional information to further your study online at www.cliffsnotes.com

D0096973

WILEY

Wiley Publishing, Inc.

Publisher's Acknowledgments

Editor
Gary Carey, M.A., University of Colorado

Consulting Editor
James L. Roberts, Ph.D., Department of
English, University of Nebraska

Production
Wiley Publishing, Inc. Composition Services

CliffsNotes™ *Mrs. Dalloway*

Published by:
Wiley Publishing, Inc.
909 Third Avenue
New York, NY 10022
www.wiley.com

1O/RS/RS/QT/IN
Published by Wiley Publishing, Inc., New York, NY
Published simultaneously in Canada

CONTENTS

Mrs. Dalloway Notes

LIFE AND BACKGROUND

Sir Leslie Stephen was fifty years old when his second daughter, Virginia, was born January 25, 1882. He had been married before, to a daughter of Thackeray, and after her death had remarried a widow with three children. He reared that family and now was in the midst of rearing one of his own. Sir Leslie was a renown literary critic, and was also a cantankerous old man, not always a pleasant father to live with. Years after her father was dead, Virginia, over fifty herself, wrote in her journal that had her father lived she would never have produced either her novels or the many volumes of essays. Her father's dominance would have prevented all creativity.

Virginia inherited her father's passion for books, and, from her mother, she inherited beauty. Virginia and her sister Vanessa were strikingly good-looking girls, their beauty being classic Greek rather than "pretty." When they were children, Henry James thought that they were unusually attractive creatures but, after they were grown, he revised his estimate. The girls were still attractive, physically, but James was shocked by their most unladylike behavior. Both girls radiated a certain demure shyness but underneath they were, like their father, out-spoken and satirical.

The Stephen children (Thoby, Vanessa, Virginia, and Adrian) were a closely-knit group and though Virginia was frail, stayed at home, and educated herself with her father's library, she was never left out of a gathering or an outing. Leonard Woolf, who married Virginia, recalls that Virginia and Vanessa were invariably together. He also recalls that when they came up to Cambridge to visit their brother, Thoby, he fell in love with Virginia immediately; many years later George Bernard Shaw wrote Virginia that she had had the same effect on him.

From the first, Virginia Stephen was unusual. Besides having James Russell Lowell as godfather, and besides being self-educated, in her mid-teens she filled a number of copybooks with original compositions, imitating first one literary style, then another. Later, after both her father and mother were dead, Virginia moved out of the family home in Hyde Park. Eventually she took a lease on a large four-storied house in Brunswick Square and rented the top floor to Leonard Woolf; she occupied the third floor; her brother Adrian lived on the second; and Maynard Keynes and Duncan Grant occupied the bottom apartment. In 1911 this arrangement was very daring for most young women but to Virginia it seemed the pleasant and practical thing to do.

Leonard Woolf had been in the Civil Service for seven years and was happy to re-acquaint himself with his old friends, the Stephens. Not surprisingly, while he was living in the apartment above his "landlady," during his leave of absence, he fell in love with Virginia all over again. He tried to prolong his leave so that he might return to Ceylon if Virginia refused his proposal of marriage but the Service demanded an answer, so Leonard decided to resign and gamble on Virginia's saying "Yes" to him. He courted her with long walks, tickets to the theater and to the ballet, but Virginia was reluctant to give him an answer. When she did agree to marry him, they made a special day of it. They took a train out from London, then hired a boat, and rowed up the river. A little over a month later, they were married.

The Woolfs spent a long and leisurely honeymoon traveling through France, Spain, and Italy, and when they returned to London they moved into Clifford's Inn, Fleet Street. It was a sooty section of London but the rooms were fine and both Virginia and Leonard felt very free in this neighborhood that had known Chaucer, Shakespeare, Pepys, Johnson, Boswell, and Tennyson. During the day Virginia worked on *The Voyage Out* and Leonard wrote *The Village in the Jungle*. In the evenings, they would cross Fleet Street and dine at the Cock Tavern.

During 1913, when Virginia was finishing *The Voyage Out,* Leonard noticed that his wife was becoming irritable and nervous. She had worked on perhaps a dozen drafts of her first novel and now that it was almost done, she was developing excruciating headaches and was unable to sleep. Leonard was not unaware that Virginia had a history of mental instability before he married her. During her childhood, Virginia suffered a breakdown, and after her mother's death in 1895 she suffered another breakdown. Now the old symptoms were recurring. For a few weeks, Virginia agreed to rest in a nursing home, but after she returned home, the delusions and sleeplessness returned, and although Leonard tried to get his wife to rest in Holford, a quiet little village where Coleridge and Wordsworth once lived, Virginia's condition remained unstable. The Woolfs returned to London, and a few days later, Virginia attempted suicide. She swallowed an overdose of veronal tablets. Four trained nurses were required during her recovery and, had it not been for Leonard, Virginia would probably have been committed. The doctors who treated Virginia during these periods of semi- and acute insanity were either ready to place her in a hospital or they were (like the doctors in *Mrs. Dalloway*) only able to suggest that she be given plenty of rest and good food. In 1913 very little was known about mental illness; nearly all cases were diagnosed as various stages of neurasthenia.

Virginia's breakdown lasted almost two years with only short periods of respite but Leonard stayed with her constantly. Meals, he remembers, would often take an hour, sometimes two. Occasionally Virginia could be induced to feed herself but often Leonard had to spoonfeed her. At times Virginia was violent, even with the nurses; at other times, she was depressed and suicidal; once she lapsed into a coma for two days.

In 1915, *The Voyage Out*, which had been held up from publication for two years, appeared. It received fairly good reviews and Virginia was cited as being an important new novelist. Immediately she began *Night and Day*. In 1917, Virginia began to return to a normal social life and it was during this time that she met Katherine Mansfield and Middleton Murry. It was also during this period that Leonard and Virginia founded the Hogarth Press. Many myths surround the Press, supposing it to have been the toy of eccentric moneyed dilettantes. Nothing could be further from the truth. The Woolfs had been living off Virginia's investments and had very little money. Leonard bought the hand press in order to occupy Virginia's mind with something manual. During 1917 and 1918, there was not a single month that she did not have reviews in *The Times Literary Supplement* and, of course, she was working on her second novel. Leonard was fearful of another breakdown. But this creative tempo was typical of Virginia's output all during her life. She always tried to keep a flow of creative writing pouring during the mornings, then, during the afternoons and in odd hours, she would write critical essays as relief and as a different sort of mental discipline.

The Hogarth Press was begun in the Woolf's dining room, with the press on the table and Virginia and Leonard teaching themselves to print by the instructions in a 16-page manual. Their first publication was *Two Stories* — one by Virginia, "The Mark on the Wall," and one by Leonard, "Three Jews." The book was entirely hand-printed, hand-bound, and sold 134 copies. Ten years later, the Press was recognized as an important publishing house and their publications' schedule was so full that the printing had to be jobbed out. During this time, the Woolfs published *Kew Gardens* by Virginia and *Poems* by T. S. Eliot (including "Sweeney Among the Nightingales" and "Mr. Eliot's Sunday Morning Service"); later the Press published another of Eliot's poems, *The Waste Land*.

The Woolfs and Eliot were close friends and it was he who suggested that, since no other English publisher would touch it, the Hogarth Press publish a large, bulky manuscript by James Joyce. Virginia and Leonard agreed to consider the manuscript, and Eliot had a friend deliver a portion of *Ulysses*. Virginia read it and thought it was raw and not particularly well-written but she did recognize a strata of genius in it, so she and Leonard promised to publish it, provided they could find someone willing to set it up in print. That was in 1918; in 1919, they had to return the manuscript. All the printers they contacted were wary of the voluminous anomaly.

The Woolfs lived in Hogarth House from 1915 to 1924. The Press was begun and became famous during the time WWI ran its course and ended. *Night and Day* appeared and received praise, but less than *The Voyage Out;* both books were financially unprofitable. In April 1920, Virginia began *Jacob's Room,* her first masterpiece. The novel concerns Jacob Flanders, a man remembered first through one person's memory, then another's. The viewpoint changes continually. It was Virginia's first successful attempt since *Kew Gardens* to fashion a multi-dimensional reality and to concoct a plot that abolished pat formulas for writing fiction. She was revealing many faces of reality when her contemporaries were insisting on a one-viewpoint, unified approach.

Jacob's Room was not an easy book to write because Virginia had no models; she was creating a new medium of narration. In addition, she was again suffering terrible headaches and insomnia and was required to spend much time in bed. She was diagnosed for lung trouble, then for heart trouble. Again the doctors suggested (as they do for Septimus Smith in *Mrs. Dalloway)* that all she needed was rest and relaxation. When she was able, however, Virginia continued to write, using a large piece of plywood with an inkstand glued to it, filling self-bound notebooks with her almost indecipherable, sharp script.

Jacob's Room was published in October, 1922, and received fiercely partisan reviews; either the reviewers thought that the novel was a poetic, electric masterpiece or else they were shocked. Virginia Woolf, the latter clique said, had defied the form of the novel: she had gone too far! They bemoaned the end of English literature. But Virginia was already working into *Mrs. Dalloway* (first called *The Hours)* and although she was upset by the bad reviews, she continued to unfold yet another impressionistically told story. Looking through her diary, one notices her excitement of being able to battle words and form and being able to do so without also having to battle mental fatigue and illness. At this time, Virginia was using the hours not spent with *Mrs. Dalloway* to write and assemble *The Common Reader,* a collection of essays about English literature. And, while writing on these two projects during 1923 and 1924, she was already planning her next novel, one to be written about her father and mother, *To the Lighthouse*.

Mrs. Dalloway, The Common Reader, and *To the Lighthouse* were all recognized as revolutionary, solid productions. The fiction was an attempt to reveal the mystery and magic of personality beneath the skin of human beings, yet it was not until after *Orlando* was published in 1928 that Virginia began to receive real monetary reward from her writings. She was 47 years old and had written for nearly 27 years. Also, it was not until *Orlando* that her work became popular with the public. The critics recognized Virginia Woolf's importance, discriminating people bought and read her novels, libraries acquired them, but the public found them difficult. *Orlando* was a breakthrough, an extravagant novel tracing the reincarnation of its main character — as various men and women — throughout the ages of English history and literature.

Following *Orlando's* success was *The Waves* (1931), a complex prose poem taking place almost entirely within the minds of its characters with a counterpoint evocation of waves and the sea; *Flush* (1933), a biography of Elizabeth Barrett Browning's dog; and *The Years* (1937), a major best seller, both in England and America, Virginia Woolf's last novel, *Between the Acts,* was published posthumously. She had finished a first draft but she was unsatisfied. No doubt she would have continued to cut and revise and polish had she lived; with all her novels she was a merciless perfectionist. But she felt her old sickness returning. During most of 1940, insomnia and nervousness grated at her, and one day in March, 1941, she wrote a note to Leonard: she felt that she was going mad and did not have the courage to battle the voices and delusions again. She acknowledged Leonard's goodness and his continuous, kind care. While she was writing the note, Leonard passed her worktable and reminded her that it was nearing lunchtime. A little later, he called to her but there was no answer. He went to look for her and found her hat and her walking stick on the river bank. She had drowned herself.

LIST OF CHARACTERS

Clarissa Dalloway

A delicate lady of fifty; the wife of Richard Dalloway.

Richard Dalloway

Quiet, gentle; holds a government post.

Peter Walsh

A former suitor of Clarissa; he is planning to marry the wife of a major in the Indian Army.

Elizabeth Dalloway

Seventeen years old; the daughter of Clarissa and Richard Dalloway.

Lucy

Maid in the Dalloway house.

Scrope Purvis

Neighbor of the Dalloways.

Hugh Whitbread

Old acquaintance of Richard and Clarissa; has a minor position at Court.

Evelyn Whitbread

Sickly wife of Hugh Whitbread.

Sally Seton

Clarissa's first close friend; now married to Lord Rosseter, and the mother of five boys.

Doris Kilman

Tutor to Elizabeth Dalloway.

Septimus Warren Smith

An ex-soldier who is shell-shocked and insane.

Lucrezia Warren Smith

Young Italian wife of Septimus.

Justin Parry

Clarissa's father.

Helena Parry

Clarissa's aunt.

Isabel Pole

Septimus' first love.

Evans

Sturdy, red-haired comrade of Septimus; killed in Italy shortly before the Armistice.

Daisy

Twenty-four years old; plans to marry Peter Walsh; has two children.

Sir William Bradshaw

A self-made man; physician to Septimus.

Dr. Holmes

A doctor whom Septimus and Lucrezia consult.

Lady Millicent Bruton

Friend of the Dalloways.

Milly Brush

Lady Bruton's secretary.

Miss Pym

Clerk in Mulberry's flower shop.

CRITICAL COMMENTARY

OUT FOR FLOWERS*

Mrs. Dalloway is not a novel that chronicles the years of the life of Clarissa Dalloway. In fact, *Mrs. Dalloway* is not a conventionally narrated novel at all. It is a collage, a mosaic portrait; it pieces together bits of Mrs. Dalloway's past and bits of Mrs. Dalloway's present on a single day—a Wednesday in mid-June, 1923. As far as plot is concerned, Mrs. Dalloway on this particular day in June prepares for and gives a party. That is all that happens. Our job is to look beyond the plot and realize who Mrs. Dalloway has been and what she has become. We must try to see

*The novel, of course, has no chapter divisions, but for the sake of discussion and easy reference, appropriate titles have been given to the various scenes.

the diversity beneath the surface of this English lady and try to get a sense of her personality. This is not an easy task because appearances deceive.

When Mrs. Dalloway was a young girl, her beau, Peter Walsh, prophesied that someday Clarissa would be The Perfect Hostess. Peter said this impulsively, out of jealous anger, yet when we finish *Mrs. Dalloway* we are left with a literal image of Clarissa Dalloway as The Perfect Hostess. Peter Walsh's chance and angry remark seems to have been most accurate. Clarissa's destiny does indeed seem to have been that of a well-bred wife who would give successful parties for her husband. This would seem to be the only value of her life.

In a sense, Clarissa Dalloway does develop into a perfect hostess; and, in a sense, *Mrs. Dalloway* is about a party Clarissa gives. But these ideas are only on the surface. A woman is never just a wife, or a mother, or a hostess; human beings cannot be defined in one word. It is only when we are ignorant, or lazy, or angry (as Peter Walsh was) that we label one another. But we make these generalized, easy assessments of people every day while knowing that we — individually — are certainly too complex to be summed up so easily. We would never dream of simplifying ourselves so narrowly because we know how very little of our "real selves" is displayed to the world. There are depths of feeling — hatred, despair, joy, sensitivity -- which are rarely revealed. And, in the same way that much of our emotions remain submerged, our minds also pile up ideas, dreams, conversations, and multitudes of words and thoughts that are never uttered. The acts we actually perform are only pale outlines of another multi-thought and -feeling individual. It is this individual which is Virginia Woolf's concern in *Mrs. Dalloway*.

Who is Mrs. Dalloway?

Probably it is best to start with what Clarissa Dalloway looks like so that we have a frame for our discoveries about her. And in determining Mrs. Dalloway's physical features we should note how we learn such details; Virginia Woolf's art of narration is just as important as the content of her novels.

We learn that Mrs. Dalloway prefers to buy the flowers herself. This seems like an innocuous statement, yet this single sentence is the entire first paragraph; it is a curious way of beginning a novel. What lies behind the first sentence is this: Virginia Woolf is getting Mrs. Dalloway out of the house so that she can be seen by strangers, by an old friend, and by a neighbor. Also, Mrs. Dalloway can react to a London she has not seen for some time. We are going to learn about Mrs. Dalloway from various points of view; we will not be told outright the facts about Mrs. Dalloway because such collections of facts reveal too little. We must learn by observation.

Mrs. Dalloway's excursion is not routine. Usually Mrs. Dalloway has things done for her; she is not used to doing errands. Today, however, seems special to her because it is fresh and brisk. The fact that the maid is busy supervising the removal of the winter doors is an excellent opportunity for Mrs. Dalloway to go out shopping. This is a day when Mrs. Dalloway is going to do something she enjoys but which, because of illness, she has not been able to do for some time: to go strolling on an errand through London's noisy, bustling traffic. The return of the summer season, the return of Mrs. Dalloway's health, and her return to a busy London scene parallel one another.

As Clarissa heads for the flower shop, we leave her thoughts and enter the mind of Scrope Purvis. Purvis has been Clarissa's neighbor for many years so his observation is valuable. He thinks of Mrs. Dalloway as bird-like — perched, as it were, on the curb. She seems bird-like despite being fiftyish and still bearing the pallor of her recent illness. She is wearing a feathered yellow hat (we learn this after she returns home) and possibly this spot of plumage influences Scrope's comparison. But, no, Clarissa also thinks of herself as bird-like — too bird-like, she would say. We learn this when she reflects on Lady Bexborough.

By comparing herself with Lady Bexborough, Clarissa (not Virginia Woolf) tells us about herself. We learn about Clarissa's physical appearance and we learn her thoughts as she compares herself with a woman whom she considers ideal. Clarissa would, for instance, gladly exchange her own pale and smooth complexion for Lady Bexborough's dark and crumpled one. She would like to have a face with more visible charcter. She would like to move more slowly and stately, not lightly; she feels that she is too flighty, too pointy-featured, and too insincere. Clarissa, it would seem, would like to be less feminine; more masculine, perhaps. At least she would like to have a more serious mien and be interested in, say, politics. She does not find her pallor or smooth skin attractive—or even natural. She talks of her body as being a "nothing" that she "wears." The only features that she approves of are her hands and feet. Otherwise, she is *not* happy with her outward appearance—the thin, white, bony sack that contains Mrs. Dalloway.

Perhaps these seem like unusual, contradictory thoughts—this despair at aging, and at aging unattractively, while Clarissa is very obviously enjoying being in the hurry and noise of the London morning. Without a doubt, Clarissa is thrilled to be in this colorful London stream; our first view of her is filled with her excited responses to being a part of the city's thoroughfare again. Her moods do alternate however; in one paragraph she is troubled and worried, in the next she is sparkling. Yet Virginia Woolf did not insert these changes of mood merely to be whimsical or lyrical.

Consider this: Clarissa's flashes of worry about aging are not at all unnatural; she has already said that she wishes she were not so delicate and brooding. Also, Clarissa has been ill, has become even more delicate, and has had too much time to think. No doubt her doctor and husband and friends commented on her looks and Clarissa would probably have consulted, first of all, her mirror as she searched for signs of illness in her over-fiftyish face. In addition, one must remember in assessing Mrs. Dalloway's fluctuations of moods that if Clarissa was confined to bed during her illness she would, like most people past fifty and confined to bed, have reflected on life. She would have recalled and pondered. Recovered now, and back in the stream of London traffic, her sick-bed seriousness would not have been immediately flushed away. There would be this natural residue of seriousness in the midst of all the wonder of this morning.

Virginia Woolf is not manipulating, for sheer effect or merely for exposition, Clarissa's present-to-past-to-present changes of mood and thought. There is valid motivation for Clarissa's ebb and flow of mood and time. The transitions are indeed swift, but our own minds can be every bit as mercurial. Human beings seem geared to clock time as it continuously moves forward, but in fact they are not. Within themselves, their minds ignore clock time and obey a different sense of time. Virginia Woolf has used Clarissa to imaginatively approximate a mind's natural course.

We discern that Mrs. Dalloway has been ill, has been resurrected, and is again enjoying the smells and sights of this busy London morning. Sharp-featured, angular-jointed, she is almost intoxicated by the noisy goings-on and, at turns, lost in thought about decisions she has made during her lifetime and about her physical shortcomings. She has been ill but has returned to the life of London and has plunged into its traffic. Now, as she makes her way up the streets, we make our own way—into Mrs. Dalloway. We have learned what she looks like from Scrope Purvis' image; then we were given Clarissa's verification. Listening to her negative comments about herself, we learned certain of Clarissa's quirks—plus one very important clue to her character. From Clarissa's minor dissatisfactions with her looks and personality grows one of the novel's major concerns: is Mrs. Dalloway satisfied being "Mrs. Dalloway"? Piecemeal, we are to learn the circumstances and the results of Clarissa's decision to become Mrs. Dalloway—this decision on a husband, the most important decision in a woman's life.

Returning to Peter Walsh, it is important to consider that we hear of him long before we hear about Richard Dalloway. This is a novel about Richard Dalloway's wife, yet it is not Richard that we learn about first; it is Peter. We discover that Clarissa, very rationally, chose to break off her relationship with Peter Walsh and, very rationally, to become Mrs. Richard Dalloway. The title of this novel and its first words are one and the same: Mrs. Dalloway. Our first impression is a double-barreled emphasis on Clarissa's married state. But already on the first page we see that Clarissa is concerned *not* with her husband, but with remembering a wry comment Peter Walsh, her former beau, made long ago as he caught Clarissa gazing into space.

The first thing we hear Peter say, as he chides Clarissa for appearing so deep in revery, is that he prefers men to cauliflowers. Peter is saying, in effect, that he prefers the company of men — of human beings — to the non-human. It is a trivial joke that Peter tossed to Clarissa, yet Clarissa's memory has preserved it all these years; and, since Virginia Woolf places it before us as Peter's first speech in the novel, it is important — a key to why Clarissa rejected Peter, why she denied herself Peter, and why still today she argues with herself that she was right not to marry Peter.

Had she married Peter, Clarissa says, he would have insisted on sharing; she then changes thoughts and recalls their break-up and the gossip she heard later about Peter's marrying an Indian woman. Even in her thoughts, Clarissa is cautious about too thoroughly considering Peter, as if even that would be too much "sharing." Clarissa is terribly fearful of the implications of sharing. As we shall see later, Clarissa equates sharing (with a man) with surrender. And Peter would have insisted on sharing an intimacy with Clarissa — and not intimacy in a sexual sense only. Peter would have insisted on a basic, defenses-down, baring-of-souls kind of intimacy — the kind of intimacy that exists between absolute friends. It was this exchange, this possession of one another's most secret depths, which frightened Clarissa. Marrying Peter would have cost Clarissa all private thoughts and feelings. This may seem to be a paltry sort of consideration but it is, in fact, more important than had Clarissa only had qualms about giving in to Peter sexually. Clarissa is considering basic communication between husband and wife — basic honesty, basic compassionate intimacy. Peter would have demanded that Clarissa release all her hopes and fears and joys to him — and he would reciprocate. This is a far more dangerous and sustained exchange than that of sex.

Dangerous, in fact, is the word Clarissa uses to describe the act of living. Were she to have chosen Peter, Clarissa would have had to lose her balance; she would have had to dare make mistakes. She chose security and safety in Richard Dalloway. Yet the spirit in Clarissa that responded to Peter, before rationality denied him to her, is still alive. In this morning's walk there is evidence of this responsive streak — one that Clarissa is still trying to discipline. As she thrills to the morning's light, sharp freshness, so like "the kiss of a wave"; as she tenses, anticipating the striking of Big Ben; and as she hears the cacophonous noise of trucks and cars and vendors magically harmonized, Clarissa scolds herself for foolishly succumbing to such sensual delight. She wonders why she loves London's bustle so.

The answer is simple: Clarissa, by nature, is responsive and spontaneous but she has learned to conceal her responses and feelings. She allows a loose rein to her senses but only in this way: London is a collection of noises, colors, smells, and people, and Clarissa can walk amidst them, can savor them, yet not have to merge with them. She can smile lovingly, and ironically, at the follies of old ladies and at the follies of young lovers, but she does so with a love that keeps its distance. She appreciates London as she might appreciate a lovely, familiar painting come to life. London — a living work of art — is like a salve to Clarissa's feeling of isolation and to the post-effects of her illness. Clarissa's doctors said that her heart might have been affected by influenza, but this is only another way that Virginia Woolf underscores for us the fact that, figuratively, Clarissa's heart has already been weakened. It was weakened by disuse long before influenza felled her. Clarissa has been too careful with her heart's affection.

Mrs. Dalloway is not a simple person. She is most complex. She is fascinating in that she realizes that her "self" changes, that it modifies to a certain degree, depending on whom she is with. With Richard, she is a little different than she is with Elizabeth; and she is different in another way when she is with Hugh Whitbread. Unlike Clarissa, most people think that they are always the same, regardless of whom they are with. In truth, few people remain constant: we all change, reacting with different parts of our personality to the many different people we spend time with.

Mrs. Dalloway also appraises people differently than most people do. When she meets Hugh Whitbread, she comments on his "well covered . . . handsome, perfectly upholstered" body. She is referring rather novelly to how Hugh's clothes fit. But, besides Clarissa's showing us a different way of looking at someone, we learn more about Clarissa. She thinks of Hugh's clothes as she thinks of her own clothes and body: as covering, distinct from the inner self under the "upholstery." This idea of a body's being upholstered is unusual and interesting, and it reinforces our notions about Clarissa's complexity. Already she has remarked about feeling "outside, looking on." She walks through life; she is inside her body, yet she feels apart from life and alien to her body. Not only does she have these feelings but she is lucid about them—and Clarissa is not a learned woman. She is not a college graduate; she has little formal education: she is merely a woman, sensitive and intuitive—with a special sensibility. Her emotions are very intense despite the fact that she would like them, like her world, to be carefully guarded and within boundaries. She would like her world of marriage and motherhood to be cool and quiet like the cool and serene park she crosses through this morning.

Matters are often beyond Clarissa's control, however. She has tried to order her life by marrying Richard Dalloway, but lately she has been near death, and lately the world has been torn by the Great War. Now both she and the world seem to be healing. The king and queen are in the palace and are giving a party tonight—just as Clarissa will be giving a party tonight. These should be happy moments—and some are—but Clarissa's joys cannot fend off certain unhappy thoughts—the intense feelings of hatred, for instance, that she has for Miss Kilman, her daughter's tutor.

Why Clarissa hates Miss Kilman is not entirely clear but already we can guess at a little: Clarissa was very ill and her daughter Elizabeth represents youth, the essence of aliveness, and the extension of Clarissa. Clarissa has never "possessed" Elizabeth, nor has Richard, but now, to Clarissa, it seems that Miss Kilman is devouring Elizabeth. This concept of owning, that was so odious about Peter's personality, has dangerously reasserted itself just when Mrs. Dalloway is growing old and the world is changing and she becoming a stranger to it.

And so, worrying about Miss Kilman, though delighting in Bond Street, Mrs. Dalloway reaches the flower shop. It has been an unusual walk. This first scene is one of great contrasts — one of active sensual excitement but also of intermittent reflection. Mrs. Dalloway has walked through the noisy streets of London, entered a quiet park, re-emerged into the noise and color, and has slipped into a peaceful, sweet-smelling flower shop. She has thought about the present, about the past, and about the present again. The back-and-forth narrative, and this back-and-forth, in-and-out current of noise and quiet have suggested the rhythm of waves, their ebb and flow. Virginia Woolf is a remarkable architect: Clarissa has already mentioned that the day felt as though it carried the kiss of a wave; she has remembered the rising and falling of the rooks — very much like waves; Big Ben booms out hours one after another, irrevocably — very much like waves; life, she says, builds up, tumbles, then creates afresh — very much like waves. In this scene and throughout the novel the changes of time, the changes of scenes, and the motif of water — the sea and the waves — are all carefully synthesized.

SEPTIMUS

While Mrs. Dalloway selects flowers for the party, we leave her for awhile and consider a new character: Septimus Warren Smith. The change of focus is brief, but it is important because Clarissa is only one half of the design for *Mrs. Dalloway*. While she worked on this novel, Virginia Woolf jotted in her diary that she wanted to sketch, in a shadowy way, "the world seen by the sane and the insane." The book was to be more than a story about Clarissa Dalloway; it would be a novel with two main characters and two stories alongside one another. The two characters — Clarissa and Septimus — never meet in the novel, yet they are linked to one another through various characters and because of the value they both give to that "leaf-encumbered forest, the soul."

Both Mrs. Dalloway and Septimus Smith are intense and sensitive—especially about the privacy of their souls—that collection of qualities which make up a personality's essence and individuality. Mrs. Dalloway has a veneered composure; she attempts to keep her most serious thoughts, dreams, and musings to herself; no one else would treasure or understand them. She restricts the boundaries of her secret world. She lives with her husband and her daughter and among her friends; she is wife, mother, and hostess, but she is never completely relaxed and open with anyone. No one sees the dark depths of Mrs. Dalloway's soul. And when Clarissa uses *dark* to describe her soul, she does not mean *dark* to connote something necessarily evil or fearful; *dark* simply means that the soul is not open for public view. Mrs. Dalloway's soul is a place of retreat, like a private garden. Perhaps this is not the healthiest attitude to take towards oneself, but Mrs. Dalloway is considered sane.

Septimus Smith, on the other hand, is insane. He has almost wholly retreated into his private world. Notice, for example, how his reaction to the noise of a car backfiring echoes and amplifies, but differs from, Mrs. Dalloway's reaction. Clarissa immediately thinks that she has heard a gun shot. There is nothing pathological about this association. The Great War is just over. An era of terrifying death and violence has officially ended, yet the fearful sounds of war remain in the unconscious. England still trembles; the sound stills the rush and hubbub of the streets.

Ironically, it was a gunshot—a multitude of them—which cut Septimus Smith's contact with reality. He is a casualty of the Great War, a victim of shell-shock. Nevertheless, he does not imagine the car's backfiring to be a gunshot. To him, the noise is the sound of a whip cracking ("The world has raised its whip; where will it descend?"). Everyone else is only startled; Septimus is terrified.

In this crowd scene of London, we have gone beyond the exterior of appearance and have had a glimpse into two private, inner worlds—Clarissa Dalloway's and Septimus Smith's. We have seen two confused and frightened people. They differ in degree, of course. Clarissa has been weakened by an illness and she is frightened and furious about Miss Kilman's "possession" of Elizabeth. But, as best she can, she attempts to keep her fears corralled and orderly. In contrast, Septimus' fears cannot be governed; they are too overpowering and chaotic. London, through Clarissa's eyes, is familiar and reassuring; for Septimus, it is only fragments of sensation. To Lucrezia, Septimus' wife, London seems totally alien. She is a stranger in a strange land, with no friends, and with a husband who threatens to kill himself.

Focusing on a simple morning scene, Virginia Woolf has challenged us with a many-prismed view: we wandered through Clarissa's wonderland of past and present thoughts; we drew back and saw the citizens of London react like one unified organism to a car backfiring; then we were jolted by the jagged reality of Septimus Smith's thoughts. Now we see what is happening through the eyes of a foreigner. So what is the "real world" like? Each person has a different idea of what truth and reality are. There is a general, agreed sense of what is true and real in a given situation but there are always highly individual interpretations. Virginia Woolf continually reminds us of such individual intricacies. One of the characters will frequently show us a sense of what is extraordinary in even the most mundane occurence. A car's backfiring is only a loud noise, yet it has unusual effects, *individually,* and it does something unusual to the *mass* of people who happen to be together on a London Street. The noise catches their attention, then the important-looking car mesmerizes them with awe. The car does not, for certain, contain anyone important, but everyone has deep veneration for it. And, from far above the story itself, we hear Virginia Woolf meditating, reflecting on the crowd's need to be associated with Greatness. The car is just a car—and even the Queen, if she be inside, is only a woman.

Yet this potent mystery takes the crowd away from its sense of being ordinary. The car endows each person with an Extraordinary Moment. Everyone feels individually distinguished because they have encountered the possibility of being in the same street with royalty, with England. We observe the blind awe of the crowd and listen to Virginia Woolf comment that only historians will know for sure who is in the mysterious car. Her attitude is like the attitude of Clarissa when, earlier, she was crossing London streets. Both women smile at the comic folly of us mortals.

The novel continues on its course as Clarissa's momentarily conferred "dignity" passes. The thought of the queen in the mysterious car reminds her of the queen's party which reminds her of her own party, and thus she is reminded once again of Peter Walsh's taunt—that she would eventually define herself as a Hostess. The pleasant, patriotic, quasi-dignity is replaced by the dread of a more sterile dignity, the dignity of a Hostess.

Suddenly our attention is drawn to something else. Something else mysterious has appeared. A plane discharging white smoke is passing overhead. The instant patriotism for Royal England that held the public spellbound only minutes before is gone—but the awe of the unknown remains. No one knew who was in the black car before; now no one knows what the sky-writing says, yet both forces have a similar compelling power over the public. The sky-writing letters form words but the message is blurred and indecipherable. What the public is watching is only an advertising gimmick, but they don't seem to recognize it as such. They are enchanted by this riddle of a commercial message in the heavens. Their attempts to read the sky-writing are wryly described, as though there were an oracular significance to the enigmatic letters.

At this point we learn that not everyone agrees that Septimus Smith is insane. Septimus' doctor, for instance, thinks that Septimus' problem is only habitual, obsessive introspection. This is Lucrezia's reason for trying to interest Septimus with the words written in the sky. But we know that Septimus *is* insane because we enter his mind and are shown the sad beauty of his madness. Time is dispersed; it is stretched, lengthened, slowed down. The smoke shapes do not mean anything to Septimus; they simply are. They are modulating colors of white, rising and tumbling.

Sounds around Septimus are amplified and richly suggestive. The movement of Septimus' sight and sound experiencings are wave-like: the smoke languishes, melts; sounds converge, then break; the light on the elm leaves rises and falls. This water imagery has been used before. It punctuated Mrs. Dalloway's morning walk and the journeys back and forth from her past to the present. The rising and falling is the rhythm of waves and it is also the same rhythm of a throb, the beat of a heart—the beat of the individual heart and the beat of our primeval mother, the sea. The rhythm beckons mightily to Septimus; the metaphorical rhythm of the great Unconscious, of the sea, is like a siren's song to Septimus' unconscious, and the remnant of his rationality fights to preserve itself. He pleads with himself that he will *not* go mad. Septimus is struggling to be the master of his own destiny, just as Clarissa is still struggling (in a parallel, though much less intense way) to be master of her destiny.

We draw away from Septimus' intense inner conflicts and Lucrezia's fears, and catch a glimpse of the Smiths from another side—from Maisie Johnson's point of view. Like Lucrezia, she is foreign to London. She is Scottish, just down from Edinburgh, and the men and women and the "prim" flowers of London—all the things that thrilled Clarissa—seem odd to Maisie. Especially odd are the Smiths, she thinks. Then we look at Maisie through Mrs. Dempster's eyes. We observe old Mr. Bently. The scene is blurring. Life has gone awry for most of the people we have met since Clarissa Dalloway stepped out of her house this morning to go shopping for flowers. The scene ends with the sky-writing airplane still noiselessly spilling blurred letters onto the sky. What do they say? They might say "toffee" but the message is still incomplete. We can interpret its blurred image any way we choose, just as Clarissa, Septimus, Lucrezia, and Maisie, Mrs. Dempster, and Mr. Bently can each decide differently about London, Londoners, and life. Human beings interpret moments of reality variously; we have seen several striking instances through the perceptions of the sane, the insane, the foreigner, the newcomer, and the elderly.

HOME AGAIN

There is scarcely any real action in this scene. Yet a few commonplace acts structure the real matter of this scene — Clarissa's thoughts about life and death. Virginia Woolf does not use these labels, of course, but they are the fundamental considerations at the core of the scene.

Already Clarissa has mulled over certain aspects of dying. Looking into Hatchards' shop window this morning, she pondered the idea that bits and pieces of herself might continue to live after she had ceased living. Also, the lines from *Cymbeline* that caught her attention concerned death; "Fear no more the heat o' the sun / Nor the furious winter's rages" is part of a funeral song. Clarissa, in the midst of noisy and colorful London, thought about death. As contrast, note what it is that accompanies Clarissa's current thoughts of death: we read that the Dalloway hall is as "cool as a vault." This is the first thing we learn about Clarissa's house when she returns home; this is our first impression. Thus there are two kinds of life to consider here: one is the busy living on the streets of London; the other kind is that which is lived within the Dalloway house. Clarissa has stepped out of the milieu of the London life and returned to her life, her sanctuary where living is, to extend the metaphor, as "cool as a vault." Virginia Woolf suggests a certain death-in-life atmosphere in the Dalloway house.

Mrs. Dalloway is aristocratic and wealthy, but one should not stereotype her; she is not a one-dimensional well-brea, well-mannered, gently religious lady. Clarissa is a lady in the old sense — but she is also an atheist. This is a surprise and thus Virginia Woolf's allusion to Clarissa's being like a nun is ironic; Clarissa is a paradox, a secular nun. Consider how Clarissa's day-to-day acts of living are performed: she does what is expected of her and whatever she does she is very orderly. Her acts are performed with the regularity of a rosary being recited. There is something holy about Clarissa's observance of day-to-day acts. But what Clarissa *seems* like, she is not *really* like. She seems nun-like, her daily acts are performed with religious devotion, yet she is an atheist. We are impressed with the irony between appearance and reality.

There is yet another contrast between the *appearance* of Clarissa Dalloway and the *reality* of Clarissa Dalloway — and it is one which Clarissa is well aware of. Clarissa realizes that her home, the Dalloway house, is a safe refuge. The house is fortress-like and sturdy, and as well-bred in its exterior appearance as Clarissa is; but, in their interiors, Mrs. Dalloway and the Dalloway house differ. Clarissa, inside, is a mass of doubts and fears. This is dramatic irony because Lucy, Clarissa's maid, worships her mistress and imagines Clarissa to be as regal and composed as she appears to be.

We see the truth of the matter when we enter Clarissa's mind. Already we have glimpsed into some of Clarissa's fears and worries; now we perceive that Clarissa is truly hurt by Lady Bruton's inviting Richard, and not Clarissa, to luncheon. Life is slipping away from Clarissa; she is frail, white-haired, and already, it would seem, is being neglected. Socially, Clarissa does not like to be snubbed by another society lady; as a female, she is jealous that Lady Bruton invited only *Mr.* Dalloway to her luncheon; and, deep down in her soul, Clarissa is stunned. Even though she does not greatly fear death, she is pained at being neglected so soon after she has been seriously ill; it is as though she were already forgotten.

We have seen that Mrs. Dalloway has secured for herself a safe, if somewhat sterile, existence. Our next matter is with Clarissa's truly "happy times." She remembers these isolated moments, fittingly, as she loosens and removes the trappings of the public Mrs. Dalloway. Up in her tower room, away from London and away from the lower rooms of the Dalloway house, Clarissa removes her hat and puts her coat away. She literally "lets her hair down." As she does so, memories of Sally Seton return. Sally was the first person Clarissa ever shared secrets and affection with. Clarissa was fascinated by Sally. Sally was everything Clarissa wasn't. Clarissa obeyed all the rules, Sally broke them. Sally sat on the floor, propped up her knees, and smoked. Once she ran naked out of the bathroom to fetch a sponge she forgot. Sally was a rebel who did the unexpected, the romantic: everything a well-bred, well-mannered young girl at the turn of the century did *not* do.

Many of us are attracted to a rebel personality, especially when we are young—and especially, we can imagine, if we had been reared, as Clarissa was, in a cloistered, Victorian atmosphere. We are told that flowers at Bourton (Clarissa's family home) were arranged in "stiff little vases all the way down the table." This is an appropriate image for Clarissa's life—because it was, until Sally appeared, made up of stiff, indistinguishable days arranged along the length of the years. Then Sally sparked Clarissa's spirit. Clarissa felt that she and Sally could "communicate."

At first, communication may seem a rather tame prize for Clarissa to value so highly, but even today our popular magazines are continually concerned with the matter of communication between people. Can men and women truly communicate? Is the male sensibility different from the female sensibility? D. H. Lawrence, a contemporary of Virginia Woolf, believed that men and women were two entirely different species. Historically, the mind of a woman has always been relegated to second place whenever a man is concerned. This was especially true when Mrs. Dalloway was a girl. In those years, whom could a girl open her heart to? A sensitive, imaginative, timid girl like Clarissa? Men were superior. If one were a woman, could she tell her husband everything she thought? If so, how would he receive it? as the confession of a silly chatterbox? or in a spirit of trust? This problem was one which frustrated Virginia Woolf. She was a published critic and author. She had many male friends, but she was prone to distrust their friendships. She wondered if she were being patronized when she talked of literature and politics. Did her male friends think of her as only a clever curiosity? Did they really "share" themselves with her as her women friends did? Was there an even exchange?

This concept of "sharing" — of giving and taking — is central to Mrs. Dalloway. Clarissa rejected Peter because he wanted to share himself and wanted an equal return. Clarissa feared open, total involvement with a man. The concept was foreign and frightening; to her, sharing meant surrender. Marriage to Peter would have been a dangerous, immoral one-sided contract. Compare, however, the give-and-take aspect of Clarissa's memory of Sally Seton. Clarissa gave her "soul" absolutely and exclusively to Sally. Sally gave her "soul" to Clarissa — but she offered, freely, just as much of herself to everyone else. When Sally kissed Clarissa, she gave the kiss impulsively. Clarissa, however, did not accept the kiss as an impulsive gesture. Clarissa accepted Sally's kiss as a treasure; she accepted it as though a ceremony had been performed and a gift had been bestowed. Nevertheless, Clarissa does not seem to see anything unjust or wrong in this disproportionate exchange.

The memory of Sally's kiss is still precious to Clarissa even though the incident happened long ago. Clarissa can remember that she thrilled in response to another human being's warmth. But *how* she thrilled? that is another matter. Her emotional response today to that memory barely registers. The memory is a keepsake, like a dead flower; Clarissa has preserved it too completely for too long, just as she has preserved a certain virginal quality about herself. Her white hair, her narrow bed, the clean tight sheets, and the book she reads about Marbot's retreat from Moscow are symbolic of the pristine, barren result of Clarissa's decision not to attempt a vital male-female relationship.

Clarissa's going upstairs is symbolic of her retreat from the challenge of living a full, adventurous life. Quiet, unassuming Richard Dalloway and his house are the principal peripheries of Clarissa's refuge but, inside the Dalloway house, there is an even safer nook for Clarissa to hide away in. This is, appropriately, the attic room. In these private quarters of hers, as in her deepest depths, Clarissa can be all alone; here she will not be disturbed, even at night by her husband.

We feel a sense of loss as Clarissa mounts the stairs and pauses midway. The soft June air and the barking of dogs flow in through an open window and remind us of what Clarissa denies herself when she nurtures and constructs protective barriers around herself. Barking dogs (fierce unpleasantness) are vanquished but then so is warm, mild June air (simple, natural happiness). And, as we shall see more clearly later, Clarissa has not really been successful in her attempt to live peacefully and harmoniously in her sanctuary. She chose to marry Richard, not Peter, to escape the "heat o' the sun" and the "furious winter's rages" — extremes of passion and unhappiness. But Clarissa did not escape entirely. Memories of Peter still fester, Elizabeth is not maturing into the image Clarissa has for her daughter, and Miss Kilman is like an awful monster that is gaining possession of Mrs. Dalloway through Elizabeth. There is a startling contrast between the public image of Mrs. Dalloway, the hostess, and the Mrs. Dalloway that Virginia Woolf shows us.

Like the dress she mends later, Clarissa shines in artificial light (the chandelier lights of parties she gives), but in real light she is revealed to be a white-haired woman beside a narrow, white-sheeted bed. In real light, Clarissa loses color — life's coloring. We watch her contemplate her image in the mirror. Like a puppetmaster, she purses the image's lips and draws the composure tightly together — concealing all jealousies, vanities, and suspicions. Clarissa composes her features, exactly as she mends her dress — drawing the folds together, arranging the folds in patterns, disguising the rents in the appearance. Back and forth, in and out, Mrs. Dalloway draws a needle through the waves of green silk. The silk, green and wavy, is reminiscent of the sea — of the vastness and the freedom of the sea. Mrs. Dalloway "plunges" her hands into it. Yet, true to form, she collects and orders the fabric — exactly as she has attempted to order the form of her life.

PETER'S VISIT

In contrast to the last scene of safe quietude, we now see Clarissa pitted against a flesh-and-blood person, one who loved

Clarissa long ago. This, incidentally, is the first vigorous male introduced to us. Clarissa did meet Hugh Whitbread in the park, but he was a rather pallid specimen of manhood — stiff, stale, and "upholstered." Now Clarissa meets her opposite — a male who lives vitally every day in his life.

Having been inside Clarissa's thoughts for so many pages, we expect her to panic when Peter arrives. Her nerves are frail and her thoughts have been fanciful and light as gossamer. We expect this reunion to be painful. It is — but not in the way we anticipate. It is Peter, not Clarissa, who suffers most in this scene. Virginia Woolf surprises us; therefore, we should consider how she accomplishes this reversal.

It is also too easy to imagine Clarissa's agony. We know that she is lost in thought . . . safe in her house . . . quietly preparing for her party. These private moments are holy. Then Peter shatters the silence of Clarissa's sewing. Of course Clarissa is inwardly furious at the bad manners of whoever has dared trespass into her home. Frightened, she even tries to hide her dress. Then she is calm. Why the change? The answer lies in the many years Clarissa has trained herself to respond like a lady — as nearly as possible — to any situation. Composure is regained and Clarissa *is* happy and excited but she continues to sew, working her needle mechanically. Judging from appearances, one would never guess the extent of Clarissa's thrill at seeing Peter. Again, there is an enormous contrast between appearance and reality. Not even Peter guesses what is happening inside Clarissa. The regularity of the motion of her sewing suggests to him that she might, conceivably, have always lived no more exciting a life than just this.

We hover above Clarissa and Peter observing the disparity between what they *think* about themselves and each other and what they actually *say* to one another. As they talk, we watch the struggles beneath the talk. At the same time that Clarissa hates Peter's silly, childish ways, she loves his adventurous qualities. She feels inadequate and inferior and needs the presence of Richard or Elizabeth to strengthen her. For his part, Peter too feels inferior. He has made no fortune and has accumulated none of the expensive things that one is expected to pile up as evidence of success. He despairs that his life has been so disorderly (full of travels, love, and work) in contrast to Richard Dalloway's undeviating years of success. What irony this is. Peter has lived a very full life yet admires values — Dalloway values — which he could not possibly emulate. And Clarissa admires qualities in Peter that she could not emulate. And how ironic it also is that Peter has come to tell Clarissa — a girl he loved long ago — that he has just recently fallen in love again. He offers Clarissa the thrill he feels about being in love — an odd gift to offer a woman who fiercely respects the privacy of feelings. Peter sits beside Clarissa exposing his secret — which, we realize, is not his love for Daisy, but his continuing love for Clarissa.

Thus we see these two old people — he, scrawny-necked but boyish; and she, white-haired and frail. They failed as lovers long ago and now they find it awkward to be friends. The conversation flares, then fades. Talk becomes touchy, so they mistakenly use the past as a crutch. The past is barbed and recalling it is like fearing open an old wound. Yet it is not the woman who breaks; it is Peter. And, above Peter's sobs we hear Clarissa, silently crying for him to take her away — meaning it, yet also not meaning it.

Later, Clarissa does call to Peter, aloud, but her attempt is pathetic. Above the roar of the open air, the traffic, and the sound of clocks striking, her offer is barely heard. These sounds — air, traffic, and clocks — are sounds of life. The rush of air, the jangle of traffic, and the noisy climax of time are far stronger than the sounds coming from Clarissa. And what, we should ask, is Clarissa offering to Peter? After he wanted to share the news of his impending marriage, what is she offering him? An invitation to a party. This is Clarissa's offer. She has offered Peter the role of guest when she will be hostess — the single role that Peter has said she would be destined (and damned) to play.

PETER IN REGENTS PARK

In general, this long scene is one of reflection. Like Clarissa, who has been ill and has "returned" to London, Peter also has been away; he is returning to London after five years spent in India. As Clarissa did, Peter sees London through unaccustomed eyes. He notices subtle nuances, and revels in being a part of, and within, a metropolis. Also, as Clarissa did, Peter considers not only present time but also past time. Especially since he has just left Clarissa, he pauses to wonder, particularly about the "success" of each of their lives. We learn a good deal more now about the circumstances of Peter and Clarissa's estrangement and also more about Peter himself. Through an interior monologue, Virginia Woolf slips us chunks of exposition and a resumé of Peter's character without ever seeming to interrupt the flow of the story.

Almost everything we learn about Peter and about the past is washed with irony. In the last scene, Clarissa imagined Peter free; she ached for freedom such as his. Here, however, we see that Peter is not as "free" as Clarissa imagines. He is free, but he is caged in loneliness. Clarissa and her set (that is, the Establishment) have rejected him. He has conformed to the requirements of his class insofar as he did go to India, "to the colonies," but he has always been an outsider. He does not, like Clarissa and Richard Dalloway, conform to the letter of the rules. When he was with Clarissa, we saw symbolic evidence of Peter's nonconformity. He played nervously with a pocketknife; he pared his nails; ecstatically, he confessed his love for a married woman. In contrast to Clarissa's conduct, Peter was not, by definition, an English gentleman whereas Clarissa, until she ran to cry after Peter, seemed the epitome of a disciplined English lady. In short, Peter has shown little social discipline.

Perhaps this is why Peter confesses to admiring the small unit of drilling soldiers: it is their discipline that is admirable. They are symbolic of war and of national greatness, but their real relevance to Peter lies in their quick-stepping, obedient uniformity—their thorough discipline. Their discipline is akin to Clarissa's. They—and Clarissa—follow rules, but Peter's nature refuses to be bridled with absolute obedience. Peter's play-adventure, for example, when he follows the strikingly good-looking woman, is a sample of his impulsive make-up. He has an imaginative bent, as does Clarissa, but Clarissa acts out her adventures within her mind. Peter puts his imagination into action. He is not content merely to dream and muse. He has teased Clarissa more than once for stargazing. True, it does seem a little mad of Peter, over fifty years old, to play at intrigue and follow the woman, but he does it on impulse. And, since this a book about sanity and madness, we might consider whether or not it really shows a touch of madness to disregard common sense and play at shadowing a glamorous, strange woman. Conversely, is it really sane to always follow *all* the rules, as Clarissa has?

We know that Clarissa is more insecure than anyone suspects. She is able to show a composed facade. But discipline has accomplished this show of strength. In truth, both Peter and Clarissa are dreadfully lonely people, entering old age, and approaching death. Clarissa has already felt the beginning of the end of her mortality but her attitude is the antithesis of Peter's reaction. Death, Clarissa tells herself, will be a time of "Fear no more," a quiet, untroubled rest. She is attempting to reckon with death rationally, as she rationally reckoned with love—and chose Richard Dalloway. She is able to admire the vitality of Peter Walsh and Sally Seton, but she married the conventional, respected Richard Dalloway. Peter is not a rational reckoner. He was unwilling to accept Clarissa's refusal to marry him and he is as equally unwilling to accept old age and the idea of dying. Clarissa's white hair and the sound of time (the iron strokes of Big Ben) weigh heavily, but he is defiant.

Peter is caught in a dilemma. He can't be like the punctual, reliable, disciplined Establishment. Yet England wouldn't be her admirable self were it not for this same Establishment. Worse, he is still very attached to Clarissa, while unable to emulate her standards. Besides this, he has never been able to basically understand Clarissa. He wonders, for instance, if Clarissa wasn't being cold and insincere when she said, "Here's my Elizabeth." He does not realize the possibility that Clarissa might have been grasping for Elizabeth. Peter's lack of little social niceties, even though they annoyed Clarissa, were signs of Peter's deep aliveness, as was his confession of new love. Peter was feeling inferior to Clarissa and she to him, yet neither knew. Then Elizabeth appeared and Clarissa grabbed for her. Peter had his "new love" and Elizabeth, at least, was Clarissa's claim to having something. Elizabeth was a desperate trump card for Clarissa.

In the interlude while Peter dozes, Virginia Woolf talks about the disparity of appearance and reality, and we have seen throughout this novel instances of this dichotomy. We have also seen how intangible and fragile the division between the two is. We have seen the multitude of "appearances" surrounding a certain reality and the illusiveness of that reality. When Clarissa was out for flowers, she said to herself that she would never say of Peter or herself "I am this, I am that." Of course, she does not strictly obey this vow, but for a moment she does gain this valuable insight. Peter too realizes something very much like these thoughts of Clarissa's. He realizes that long ago he knew why Clarissa annoyed him, why he was repulsed by her while at the same time loving her. Several times already he has said variations of "still, there it is" — about situations which are ridiculous and contradictory, yet — at their core — painfully human.

This realization of Peter's is that irony and ambiguity inevitably accompany most human relationships. Both Peter and Clarissa have, individually, considered and decided about the death of Clarissa's soul. Clarissa was sure that she was saving her soul when she chose to renounce Peter and marry Richard; Peter is sure, even today, that the death of Clarissa's soul began the moment that Clarissa married Richard Dalloway. In so many ways we saw that Clarissa and Peter were able to talk to one another without verbal communication, yet about this all-important point — Clarissa's soul — their ideas are antithetical.

There is also irony surrounding Peter's and Charissa's confessions of love. The day Clarissa rejected Peter is in vivid juxtaposition to the scene just finished at the Dalloway house. Earlier we saw Peter telling Clarissa about his new-found love, a married woman with children; now we see how Clarissa told Peter of her affection for Richard. Never before had Clarissa been so open and free with him. Peter, however, insisted later on Clarissa's pronouncing the truth about herself and Richard. He wept then and he wept today. He called after Clarissa then just as she called after him today. But above all other of the impressions we have about Clarissa and Peter, there is a strong pervading sense that in spite of Peter's "love" and Clarissa's "security" that each of them is still lonely for the other. When we left Clarissa calling after Peter, the mood was one of agonized loneliness. And Peter is in love, and should be happy, yet he is not.

This mood of loneliness is used as a transition. Septimus and Lucrezia Smith come into our focus. They are with Peter in the park and both of them, like Clarissa and Peter, feel isolated from one another. Like Clarissa's being unable to understand Peter's social ineptness, Lucrezia cannot understand Septimus. It seems to Lucrezia that her husband should not "act like that." Clarissa disapproved of Peter's actions; Lucrezia disapproves of Septimus' actions—but the contrast is enormous: Septimus is insane and losing his hold on life; eventually he will toss it away. Peter has never abandoned life.

Peter of course never guesses what we know about Rezia and Septimus. And Rezia never guesses at the multitude of confusing thoughts simmering inside that "kind-looking man," as she describes him. Peter sees Rezia and Septimus and thinks that young people are freer than he was as a youth. But Peter and Sally Seton, although they were not in love with one another, were very free and candid with one another. And Rezia and Septimus are *not* young lovers and their quarrel is far more serious than a simple lovers' quarrel.

The sun is lulling Peter; he is basking in a brief, lazy luxury of blaming the times for his troubles. It has been a long interior monologue; Peter has tried, and failed, to fit all the pieces of the past into the empty spaces of the present.

THE DOCTORS

The Smiths are still here in the park and, by bringing Peter to the park, Virginia Woolf provides a seemingly chance link between the two narrative threads of the novel — Clarissa's story and Septimus' story. Peter does not speak to the Smiths, nor they to him; in passing, they merely observe one another. The linking of Clarissa to Septimus, via Peter, is frail but Virginia Woolf is structuring each world — Clarissa's and Septimus' — linking them as if by chance. Later in the novel, again as if by chance, the two worlds will collide: Septimus' death will intrude upon Clarissa's party.

Up to now, Virginia Woolf has incorporated interior monologues, scenes from past and present, brief conversations, and lyric interludes into her narration; there have been few passages which could be called directly expository. Midway in her novel, however, she inserts this long section dealing with Septimus Smith — why he is insane and how his wife deals with his insanity. During the first half of the book, Clarissa (and Peter, to a lesser degree) has been stage center and the Septimus scenes have seemed only distant, distilled echoes of the lonely Clarissa-Peter situation. Virginia Woolf has pieced together the riddle of Clarissa's isolation very artfully, but she deals differently with Septimus' situation. We are told starkly what Septimus did before the war and his madness is not explained in depth. One might naturally think that the techniques used to tell Clarissa's story might lend themselves more readily to exploring Septimus' insanity but Virginia Woolf makes a reversal. This insane situation is described almost clinically and Septimus' insanity becomes all the more horrifying thereby.

The war destroyed Septimus Smith: Virginia Woolf makes this point clear. One of the first things that we should be concerned with is what, exactly, was destroyed. Before the war, Septimus was absentminded, or at least he did not care enough about social amenities to observe them. Like Peter's playing with his pocketknife in public, Septimus neglected washing his hands. These are small matters but Virginia Woolf's style is sparse and suggests by these hints that each of these men had a streak of the rebel in him. Peter was a romantic, open, adventurous man; Septimus was a poet. He stammered, lectured on Shakespeare, did not take care of his health, kept irregular hours, and had a wistful, poetic love affair with a Miss Pole. He was thoroughly undisciplined. To his employer, he appeared to have a serious lack of manly, commercial initiative.

It was the war which, in the opinion of those who knew and worked with Septimus, made a man of him. Yet Septimus had no real grasp of what he was doing when he volunteered for the war. Virginia Woolf insists that Septimus Smith's England was not the England of most soldiers. His England existed only in literature. It was *not* to save an economically and politically distressed island that Septimus went forth to war.

Septimus himself, for a time, became proud of his manly non-emotional reaction to military carnage. He faced death and did not flinch: this was what it meant to be a mature man. Before the war, Septimus had been a disciple of literary romance; during the war, he was converted to the popular romance of the brave, undaunted hero one sees on recruiting posters. Ironically, the war did *not* metamorphose Septimus into a man: the war emasculated Septimus. It left him in horror of himself. He was a tragic casualty—a walking corpse because he could not care any longer what happened to himself or anyone else. His capacity for compassion was destroyed and he is very conscious of what has been lost.

The paragraphs Virginia Woolf devotes to Septimus shimmer. The broken pieces of his intellect and imagination turn like a mobile of wind chimes, changing colors, turning, reflecting whatever brushes them. He and Rezia are as different as a wildly abstract painting and a primitive domestic scene. Rezia is at a loss to know why her English husband is so complex; all she wants is a happy home and babies. Thus she calls in the doctors. As a simple person, she believes that there must be a simple solution to Septimus' problems.

The doctors in this scene are monstrous. Virginia Woolf is bitter in her portrayal. One, Holmes, is a professional ignoramous and a lecher; he is a smiling villain. He thinks Septimus cannot really be ill because there is no germ. But he continues to treat him because he enjoys ogling Rezia. If Holmes is ineffectual, however, Sir William Bradshaw is even worse. He recognizes that Septimus is on the verge of a nervous collapse but he is eager to experiment with Septimus. Ironically, *he* is an unfeeling doctor, the very worst type to help Septimus. He does not really care about Septimus, and yet Septimus' concern about his own inability to care has driven him insane. Bradshaw, like the soldiers Peter saw drilling, is an example of what rigid discipline can produce. He meticulously trained himself, crossed social class barriers, and emerged inhuman—full of platitudes, stock optimism, sterile knowledge, and an aggravating sense of inferiority. Bradshaw wants power; he demands that his patients be absolutely submissive. Ironically, Rezia brought Septimus to the doctors so that Septimus' alienation could be cured; she is even more alienated from her husband when the scene ends and soon the doctors will demand that Septimus be physically separated from her.

AT LADY BRUTON'S

Halfway through *Mrs. Dalloway*, Richard Dalloway makes his first appearance. However, he is still not our main concern. Virginia Woolf is far more interested in showing us Lady Bruton and, to a lesser degree, Hugh Whitbread, than she is in introducing us to Clarissa's husband. In her diary, Mrs. Woolf wrote that she wanted to criticize the social system in this novel. Here, in the character of Lady Bruton and Hugh Whitbread, she makes a critical jab. In the preceding scene, she exposed Holmes and Bradshaw's slavish devotion to appearances; here she uses an entire scene to gently ridicule certain English manners. The small luncheon party scene is a foretaste, a minature of the later, climactic party scene. It shows us the hypocricy, the fear, and also the boredom which are beneath the surface of social amenities.

Virginia Woolf satirizes English pomp and stuffiness. As the scene begins, Lady Bruton is presented as monied, imperious, and brusque; by the time the scene is over, we have watched Lady Bruton weaken, grow fearful, and become downright obedient. Hugh Whitbread appears to be a milquetoast, but he is brutish in that he is robot-like—a specimen of super discipline. He has no imagination and little emotion; he has followed all the right roads, said all the right things, and, unlike Peter Walsh, he has never been caught in a social *faux pas*.

In contrast to Clarissa Dalloway (who admires but admits feeling inadequate next to Hugh), Lady Bruton does *not* admire Mr. Whitbread. He is able to impress Clarissa with a sense of sound money, gentle birth, and impeccable breeding, but Lady Bruton thinks of him as decidedly ill-bred. The only crack in Lady Bruton's polished manner is her inability to write well. To fill this deficiency she is dependent on a master of disciplined form, social and rhetorical: Hugh Whitbread. It is little wonder that, because her illustrious ancestors were responsible for vision and victory in Britain, she is pained at being dependent on this perfectly turned, un-human cog. But Lady Bruton is not the only one dependent on Hugh. So is Peter; Hugh already expects that he will have to write a letter of recommendation for Peter Walsh.

Besides revealing that sterility and sham lie under certain social manners, Virginia Woolf is also linking her "tunnels," as she calls them, that she is digging beneath each of her characters. All three of these people—Lady Bruton, Hugh Whitbread, and Richard Dalloway—were on the periphery of Peter and Clarissa's love affair. The past again intrudes on the present; no one at the luncheon party has forgotten Peter's passionate love for Clarissa. This germinates a vow in Richard Dalloway—one that he will repeat, in vain, to himself numerous times—that he *will* tell Clarissa that he loves her.

RICHARD AND CLARISSA

Clarissa Dalloway's character was introduced to us in fragments; but the pieces were large and began to fit together rather easily. Our introduction to Richard, on the other hand, has existed only in very small fragments so far—as an instant in memory (Clarissa's) or in contrast to another character (Peter Walsh). In this scene, the fragments fasten themselves to a large, chapter length portrait, and we finally meet the man Clarissa preferred to Peter Walsh.

Certainly Virginia Woolf has nursed our curiosity about Richard Dalloway. Peter Walsh has told us a few things about him, as has Lady Bruton, but sometimes one person's comments about another will reveal infinitely more about himself than about the other person. Peter's judgment, for example, that Richard would be far happier in Norfolk than in London, should be held in suspension until we hear or have verification from Richard himself; it's possible that Peter could have been rationalizing. As it turns out Peter's intuition was accurate; Richard *is* nostalgic for Norfolk. He is not merely the vague English official that has been suggested by various hints. He is sensitive to the feel of the wind, the color of the sky, and the movements of grass. He is like Clarissa in this respect. But, unlike Clarissa, he is not resistant. Clarissa resists too-active sensual experiences and active male-female relationships, where Richard is more pliable, both with Clarissa and with a stuffed shirt like Hugh Whitbread. Richard's pliability is seen in the manner in which he acquiesces to Clarissa's needs and notions about the temper of their marriage, and because he is naturally amiable, he gives in to Hugh's whims.

Here Virginia Woolf shows us a situation in which Richard is aware that Hugh is a prig and poseur yet follows him into the jewelry store anyway. Therefore we realize that Richard lets Hugh make demands of him, just as he lets Clarissa make demands of him. In other words, Richard lets himself be carried along. And thus by characterizing Richard in this way, Virginia Woolf moves imperceptibly from character to motif. She speaks again of tides and seas and we realize that wave-like, scene by scene, we—and the characters of this drama—are being carried along toward the shore, where the party will climax the novel. Then all will recede—back into the past, back into the sea, back

42

into memory. Throughout this novel, Virginia Woolf has taken us on toward the party, inserting the sound of clocks as they marked off the end of one wave, one moment of this day, then merged us into the next moment to carry us farther.

In this scene in the jewelry shop, while Hugh is being a pompous boor about a piece of Spanish jewelry, we note a difference between Richard Dalloway and Peter Walsh. Peter is a romantic, he follows dreams, and he also follows people (the girl on the street), but he made the girl the object of a playful quest. Richard Dalloway also follows people, but he follows them doggedly. He is not very romantic, in either an adventurous or an amorous sense. His thoughts about a present for Clarissa are tainted with apology and fear. He has never been successful with his gifts to her; he does not dare actually buy jewelry for Clarissa. Instead he chooses flowers. Flowers, of course, are lovely and thoughtful. But only a few pages back, we saw another man offering flowers to a woman: Hugh Whitbread gave them to Lady Bruton: he gave them to his hostess. Now Richard will reject the idea of jewelry and decide on a gift of flowers and present them to Clarissa, another hostess. Virginia Woolf's sense of irony is keen.

Richard chooses flowers because they can be given, and accepted, impersonally. He dares not break a certain silent compact between himself and Clarissa and make any situation too personal. Clarissa did not dare marry Peter Walsh; Richard does not dare buy too personal a present for Clarissa. He is hesitant about daring to really love her, just as she was hesitant about daring to love Peter Walsh. Richard's fear of crossing Piccadilly, while several children nonchalantly scamper across, is indicative of this timidity. He has lost a life in the country by marrying Clarissa; she let herself lose Peter Walsh. Clarissa fled to Richard and has infected him with certain of her fears. He must now observe certain rules of behavior with his wife if he is to preserve their untroubled union. When Virginia Woolf says that Richard carries his flowers "as a weapon" as he crosses the park and approaches the female vagrant, she intends for us to understand that he also carries the flowers as a weapon against saying the unsaid "I love you" to his wife. He is afraid to be natural and impetuous. How paradoxical that flowers – natural and beautiful – should be a substitute and a defense against the natural and beautiful "I love you."

When we compare Richard's arrival with Peter's earlier arrival, we find that Clarissa is upset in both scenes. She is not, however, upset by Richard as she was by Peter. Invitations, obligations, and Elizabeth's relationship with Doris Kilman vex her – but Richard does not. In fact, she does not even respond, initially, to Richard. She responds to the flowers. Their relationship, in this first scene together, seems almost as empty as the drawing room with its chairs moved back against the wall. For a few minutes, like the flowers "at first bunched together," Clarissa talks quickly about Hugh and Peter, and Richard talks quickly about Hugh and Lady Bruton; then, like the flowers, the two people begin "starting apart." And Richard must be off – separating – like the flowers.

When Richard is gone, Clarissa thinks him silly for wanting her to follow the doctor's orders, but this is quite in keeping with what we have seen of Richard. He follows doctors' orders because he follows Clarissa's own unspoken orders. He respects and observes the gulf Clarissa wishes to remain between them. She tells herself that she "loves her roses" more than the Albanians Richard has gone to confer with and we recall Peter Walsh's long-ago taunt that he preferred people to cauliflowers. What is important to Clarissa: people or cauliflowers?

She says she likes life so we must consider what her sense of life is. At her parties people gather and talk and this satisfies Clarissa. For herself, she has created a life-situation. Can we condemn her for her definition of life? For she is not just a cold, cocktail party hostess; we know that. We have seen that she is responsive to the poetic and to the imaginary; her impressions of atmosphere, people and time are most sensitive. But we must also realize too that parties are arranged situations. There is little that is natural or spontaneous about them until cocktails have warmed the cold contact between the guests. People wear their best faces and best manners to parties. They keep one another at a certain social distance. Of course Clarissa enjoys party situations with their observed, good-mannered, friendly distances. This metaphysical distance around one is what supremely matters to her. Parties are Clarissa's gift; these are her own words — *her gift* — meaning her special talent — and her special present to life.

ELIZABETH AND HER TUTOR

It is far more interesting to consider the tutor, Miss Kilman, than it is to consider Elizabeth Dalloway. Perhaps this is true because Virginia Woolf, like Milton and many other writers, produces *tour de force* creations in her villains. And certainly Miss Kilman *is* a villain — and a magnificently created one. She is the counterpart of the doctors in the Septimus scenes; they are after Septimus' soul, she is after Clarissa's.

When Mrs. Dalloway was out for flowers this morning, she thought of death — and tried not to fear it; it seemed to promise an end to fearing. Far more than death, we realized when the scene was ended, Mrs. Dalloway fears Doris Kilman. She thinks of the tutor as a tyrant, as a blood-sucking, nocturnal spectre. A monster, she calls her, with "hooves" that threaten "that leaf-encumbered forest, the soul." She is like a heathen invader and it is apropos that when we first meet Miss Kilman she is on the landing, outside Clarissa Dalloway's door. She is outside the Dalloway's social class — and fiercely jealous of their easy manners, their money, and their position. She is a bulky, mackintoshed bundle of hate and self-deception.

Doris Kilman's self-deception has two poles — the secular and the sacred: concerning the first, she was hired to teach history to Elizabeth, theoretically a subject for objectivity, but Miss Kilman lacks all sense of objectivity. She is convinced she has a right to all that the Dalloways possess. Why? For one reason: because she is poor. Her reasoning is that Mrs. Dalloway does not deserve money or social position because her life has been full of vanity and deceit. If this were true, however, Miss Kilman could not logically claim the Dalloway prize either because she herself is fiercely vain. She is a reverse snob. She wears her old, smelly mackintosh as a proud insignia—to show that she is poor and that she is not trying to look as though she belongs to another, higher, social class. The impression is fraudulent.

Miss Kilman's other pole of self-deception, her sacred dimension, is her main source of strength—and hate. She has turned to religion for solace and peace but does not realize that she is actually waging a small-scale holy war against Clarissa Dalloway. She gives herself absurd grandeur by comparing her suffering in life with Christ's agony. Like the church, she is dogmatic, and like all invaders who wage holy wars, she is terribly self-righteous. She is after Clarissa's soul, the goal of the church, and also the most sacred, individual possession of Mrs. Dalloway. Ironically, Clarissa feared males, rebelling against their tradition-conferred domination. She idealized the natural, easy comradeship of "women together." Yet here, in Doris Kilman, is a monster far more terrifying than any man in Clarissa's life. And, though we see that Clarissa can face Miss Kilman in the flesh, it is the *idea* of Miss Kilman that terrifies her—the vulgar, envious, destructive force that, like a serpent, has slipped into the Dalloway house and threatens to poison and destroy Clarissa.

Miss Kilman, the sweaty, mackintoshed tutor, looks like a nobody; no one would guess the degree of frustrated possessiveness seething in her: if only she can gain Elizabeth, she will have succeeded, as a first step, in conquering Clarissa Dalloway. Her appearance successfully disguises her goal. But Virginia Woolf shows us Doris Kilman's real nature. When, for example, Miss Kilman is eating in the restaurant with Elizabeth, we see her eating "with intensity"—greedily gobbling down the pink sugared cakes and consuming the chocolate eclairs. Ugly, plain Miss Kilman is trying to devour Clarissa Dalloway and Elizabeth. She is hungry for Clarissa's loveliness, for Elizabeth's youth, for money, poise, and class—and the cakes and pastries will never sate her. As she stuffs the delicacies into her mouth, we notice her hands. They open and close, the fingers curling inward. It reminds us of the convulsive, spreading claws of a cat who is intent on its prey.

Virginia Woolf does not leave us with thorough hatred for Doris Kilman, however; she draws us back and gives us the distance to pity this thwarted creature. Her last words, in fact, as she calls after Elizabeth are "Don't quite forget me." They are very much like the words Clarissa called after Elizabeth as she left the house, "Remember the party." Both women, Clarissa and Doris, are frightened of loneliness. Clarissa's parties are her restorative, but Miss Kilman has no such solace, not even in the church. She feels that Clarissa has won and that she has lost. Her love for Elizabeth and her hate for Clarissa have torn her apart.

Clarissa, on the other hand, fears that Doris Kilman has won the battle for Elizabeth. Neither woman, we realize, has won thus far. If Elizabeth belongs to anyone, which is doubtful, it might be her father. Like Richard, she is pliable. She allows Miss Kilman to dominate much of her time, just as Richard allows Hugh Whitbread to corral him into the jewelry shop. And, also like her father, she prefers being in the country to London. Parties tire her and compliments are beginning to bore her. She is, according to her class, disciplined; so she returns punctually for Clarissa's party. But Elizabeth has not begun to really either live or love yet. She is only at the brink of adulthood. What will Elizabeth eventually be like? It's impossible to say because in addition to being like her father, she is carrying her mother's sense of privacy. She daydreams of helping other people, but it is as the mistress of a grand manor that she sees herself — making the rounds, checking on the health of the workers. It is a silly, adolescent ideal but it does contain this kernel: she would help others, she would love — but from a distance, a social distance, in this case, but still a distance.

THE SUICIDE

Of all the novel, Virginia Woolf found it hardest to write Septimus' mad scenes. She herself had suffered long periods of insanity and it was painful to recall the visions and the sounds she hallucinated. These scenes, however, besides containing the ruins of a lyric, poetic mind, are some of the most concrete in the novel. There is a terrifying sense of what it is like to be insane, to have one's mind lucid one moment, displaced the next. Solids become liquids, lights become shadows, colors glow and fade. The change from moments of sanity to moments of insanity follow a rhythmic ebb and flow, a rhythm already noted which is much like a continuing heartbeat behind the actions of the novel. The sound and the sense of the sea is continually with Septimus — and especially in this section.

Septimus' feeling of being very far away is akin to Clarissa's feeling early this morning as she strolled through London. His "Fear no more" is her comfort. From what he has dictated to Rezia, he seems to have come to terms with death, a subject which has also been on Clarissa's mind. His "there is no death" is very similar to Clarissa's belief that bits of her self will continue after she is gone, becoming parts of trees, air, people, water. Indeed, the touch of the neurotic in Clarissa, and in the other characters, is paralleled and condensed into madness in Septimus. As Miss Kilman has just done, he cries out against human cruelty. Yet Septimus is not cruel. People who dominate are cruel — whether it is within the drama of war or of single personal relations. In Septimus' case it is both. The war destroyed him; now the doctors have come to feed on him. "Holmes is on us," he says. Miss Kilman is after Clarissa's soul, but Clarissa has prized her soul for a very long time; she married to protect it and has built social and psychological barriers around it. Septimus was broken by the violence of war and can no longer defend himself — nor can the lonely, foreign Rezia defend him. Doctor Holmes has come to invade Septimus' most private depths; like Miss Kilman, Holmes and Bradshaw are obsessed with what Clarissa and Septimus fear most: possession. The opponents of Clarissa and Septimus are all from classes lower than the best, but they have been granted admittance through perseverence, education, and employment. They do not demand equality in the new class; they demand domination. Septimus characterizes Holmes as having red nostrils and as "snuffing into every secret place."

This is very much like the descriptions of the monster, Miss Kilman, who threatens Clarissa Dalloway. Both Miss Kilman and Dr. Holmes believe that they have a *right* to their victims.

Septimus' last words, "I'll give it you," are ironic. Since Holmes intends to carry Septimus off, Septimus gives himself — that is, his physical body — to the doctor. But his soul he refuses to give up. He leaps out to preserve, through death, the privacy of himself. Holmes calls Septimus a coward, but his name-calling smacks of a villain's "Foiled!" Holmes cannot understand why Septimus has jumped, but for the first time Rezia understands her husband.

BEFORE THE PARTY

The first sentence in this scene is transitional, linking Septimus' suicide — a major occurrence — with a random observation that Peter Walsh makes. The speed and the noise of the passing ambulance suggest to Peter one of the "triumphs of civilization." This is nothing more than a commonplace, a pause to appreciate the scientific mind and its achievement. Yet in the preceding scene we were concerned with the same subjects — science and triumph. The scene ended, however, not with the scientists' triumph but with Septimus' triumph. He refused to submit; his "self" was precious; he believed in its sanctity and its mystery; and he died to preserve that mystery. There is irony in Peter's speaking of efficiency and organization so soon after Septimus' suicide, as there is irony in Septimus' receiving no respect when he was alive while the ambulance, possibly carrying his mangled body, prompts Peter's respect.

Peter's marveling at the invention of the automobile recalls the fascination of the townspeople for the black limousine early in the novel. Men are dazzled by things, by titles on people, by skywritings, but they approach one another with closed minds, pre-judgments, and scientific curiosity. Too often they are devoid of awe for the greatest miracle of all: the diversity and the mystery of the human personality. Certainly our own appreciation for the human mind becomes enriched as we read this book. Virginia Woolf offers us the human personality in its most disciplined sanity and in its most chaotic insanity.

As Peter continues to reflect, his observations are echoes of ideas we have already been concerned with. The idea of life and death merging and coming together are forces at work within Clarissa, as they were within Septimus. When Peter identifies his flaw as his "susceptibility," we remember that Clarissa also shares this flaw. Both have skeins of naked nerves; both are vulnerable to beauty, both register sensitive insights into life, yet Clarissa has sheltered her flaw within Richard Dalloway's gentle protectiveness. Peter has no such refuge from reality. He has never been able to disguise or master his intensities—but then he was not able to master Clarissa either; she feared too much the conjunction of their susceptibilities.

Clarissa's idea this morning about people not really dying but becoming part of other people takes on another meaning now. As the day of Wednesday, June 23, has passed, Virginia Woolf has caught moments, touched them with water imagery, and offered them to us as happening before our eyes. But do they fade and die? No, they become part of many people's memories; they become like snapshots imprinted on the leaves of memory. They will blur, but they will be waiting for a place or a phrase to recall them.

Consider the memory-snapshots Peter takes out tonight. They once were "moments" too, unfamiliar moments to us; Clarissa, breathless, on the upper deck of a bus, babbling to Peter; Clarissa in the country; Clarissa on a hilltop, pointing, her cloak blowing out; and Clarissa, spontaneous, arguing, discussing. True, Clarissa while walking through London this morning recalled plunging into the spring air when she was a girl, but the Clarissa we see very frequently straightens herself upright when she feels herself physically, or mentally, slumping. Her imagination soars and plunges, but what of the woman herself? This Clarissa has avoided spontaniety between herself and Peter, and between herself and Richard. Does Peter see, then, the Clarissa we have seen in our moments with her? Or does he see another Clarissa beyond the white-haired, beak-nosed woman we watched mending her sea-green dress? We cannot but like Peter's memories of Clarissa. The Clarissa he is in love with, the young girl on the hill, is a captivating creature — twinkling, a bit of a nymph, thoroughly lovely. How often, we must wonder, was Clarissa like the girl he remembers? Has his memory been idealized, colored with his own imagination? For Peter *is* imaginative. Even now he is imaginatively trying to re-create what was happening within Clarissa as she wrote the letter he receives.

Abruptly Virginia Woolf moves us into Daisy's mind. We see Peter through Daisy's eyes and *he* becomes different from the man we know as Peter Walsh. Daisy sees Peter as having reserves, as being a bookish gentleman, and as being the best judge of cooking in India. Again Virginia Woolf is showing us the variety of selves that inhabit a human being under the guise of a single name. It would seem that Peter does not toy with his pocketknife when he is with Daisy, as he does with Clarissa; nor does he sob uncontrollably with Daisy. The man Daisy describes sounds more like Richard or Hugh. Daisy evokes certain attitudes and responses from Peter; Clarissa evokes entirely different facets of Peter's personality.

And what kind of a marriage will Peter and Daisy have? More than likely, paradoxically, Peter's thoughts lead us to believe that it might become a marriage very much like Clarissa and Richard's. With Clarissa, Peter, although in his fifties, is like a young boy responding to the young girl in Clarissa that he knew and will always remember. With Daisy, Peter is fiftyish. Note how conservative he is about this marriage, compared to the one he had hoped for with Clarissa. He considers the quiet of being alone, and of being "sufficient to himself." These attitudes are foreign to his relationship with Clarissa, yet they are what he is contemplating after he marries the 24-year-old Daisy.

Peter is lonely as the scene ends. This theme pervades the novel. The strangers whom Peter meets at dinner do their best to establish a satisfying link, through small talk, with Peter. Peter has tried to re-establish a link with Clarissa; he has thought about the links he is forging with Daisy. People go to parties to link together, to not be lonely. People give parties to offer the opportunity for other people, for a moment, to link; for a moment, not to be lonely.

THE PARTY

Like the birds on the curtain that blows back and forth during the party, we flit in and out of the party. First we are in the mind of one of the guests, then we are above and listening to that guest speak; we note incongruities, Virginia Woolf's satiric touches, then move on to another guest. The pace is fast, the tempo is party-like. Out of scraps and impressions, this scene is constructed to give us the noise, the smells, the rhythm of a party, and to give us omniscience. We note the mannered fraudulence and dramatic ironies. Most of the novel's cast are here, brought together for a moment in time, as Virginia Woolf ties together the narrative threads of her novel.

Among some of the incongruities and dramatic ironies, we note Elizabeth Dalloway wearing the necklace her father gave her. Her mother, remember, has never been satisfied by Richard's choice of jewelry; Richard gave Clarissa a bracelet once but she has never worn it. And, while on the subject of Elizabeth, note that while she is standing, elegantly and handsomely adorning the party as the Dalloways' daughter, she radiates composed loveliness: she knows she does. People compare her to a lily or a willow: she knows they do. Yet she never betrays her lack of interest in her mother's party or her continuing concern over her dog, which has been shut up for the evening. We see surface impressions, then dive inward and see an entirely different sort of reality. Virginia Woolf has continually taken us backstage. And it is literally backstage that we begin the party scene. This section begins with the maids bustling and worrying. Foods are described and the comedy among the cooks and the servants is recorded; the party preparations are solid support for Virginia Woolf's impressionistic style; they anchor the scene and give it balance. Then, besides cleverly taking us through the kitchen before we are admitted to the party, Virginia Woolf slyly slips in Peter Walsh's entrance to the party. It would be easy to overlook his entrance for he is included with several "Lords" and "Ladies" and "Sirs" and only his last name is announced by Wilkins.

Some of the irony in this scene is tender, like the differing responses of mother and daughter to Richard's gifts of jewelry. But most of the irony is wry. We are sure that Clarissa will manage her party most efficiently but, at its beginning, she has a bad case of nerves. Clarissa is timid, sure she will be awkward, and sure that Peter can spot the cracks in her composure. Her frustration is therefore piled on Ellie Henderson, whom Clarissa considers a bore. Ellie is standing alone, like a dolt, but inside she is as unnerved and panicky as Clarissa. Likewise, Lady Bruton assumes a regal air, yet we learned at her luncheon that parties terrify her. In fact, strangely, the person who seems to be most enjoying the party is Richard Dalloway. He talks easily to the titled guests, eases Ellie's terror, and is truly delighted to discover and talk with Peter Walsh. Richard is far more at ease than his wife. Clarissa, the hostess, of course, recalls Peter's taunt. Her fears remind us that Peter has as much as said that she would turn into a wooden, party-giving robot.

Certainly Clarissa is not robot-like, but the one thing Clarissa has done with her life is give it design. She has tried to make her life sane and safe; she realizes that it does have a certain wooden quality. And we realize this fact even more thoroughly when Sally Seton appears. Sally is still a good deal like Peter. Neither one follows the rules if they choose not to. Sally comes to Clarissa's party without an invitation. Peter burst in on Clarissa unexpectedly earlier in the afternoon. Both were, and still are, impulsive people. Sally is sure that Clarissa disapproves of her marrying a self-made man and having five sons. And Peter, by the same token, is sure that Clarissa disapproves of his never having gotten rich or obtaining a really fine position. Yet both are still fascinated with Clarissa — and she is still fascinated by each of them. Why? Perhaps for that answer we must return to our original question: Who is Mrs. Dalloway?

We realize the futility of answering such a question. It is a question that Virginia Woolf tried not to answer with a portrait, but with a novel-as-sketch. Human beings, she knew, are mixtures. So is the present—and the past. Within themselves, human beings are composed of *their* concepts, *their* memories, and *their* presents; and, in the eyes of other people, the same human beings are composed of another set of impressions, emotions, and distortions. To get a true sense of Clarissa Dalloway, one must not look for a clearly outlined, traditionally dimensioned reproduction of a fictional character. The pieces of Clarissa which Virginia Woolf has given us do fit together, but each person's impression of Clarissa must be considered as being separate, yet valid; then if we realize this, and draw back and see the novel as a sketch, as shadowy, as a series of gestures, and not as a complete, composed picture, we see a work of art far more exciting and multi-dimensional than had the author merely created a conventional figure in a conventional plot.

The novel ends as Clarissa is approaching Peter. We end by observing Clarissa Dalloway, along with Peter, as he says, "there she was." We see multiple images; we see the mystery, the variety and the richness of a human being who is far more than a hostess. We are particularly aware of the mystery because the spirit of our age is scientific and too often we expect when we finish a book to say, "I know all about that character." One cannot say that about Clarissa Dalloway. We have continually seen how different people interpret what they see and what they hear.

Who is Mrs. Dalloway: Is she the girl on the hilltop who, within Peter's memory, will remain forever on the hilltop, pointing toward the river? Is she the plumed bird Scrope Purvis saw perched stiffly on the curb? Is she the vain, emotionless *grande dame* whom Doris Kilman sees? Is she the recluse in the tower room? Is she the frail white-haired lady, mending a dress, crying silently for Peter to take her away? Is she the young girl Sally Seton impulsively kissed? Is she the flower-buyer, deeply and deliciously inhaling the sweet odors of lilacs and roses? Is she the generous, composed lady that Lucy the maid sees? To the doctors, would she be a latent Lesbian who is frigid and harboring paranoid tendencies? Is she a complete stranger, yet someone who knows more thoroughly than even Rezia why Septimus committed suicide?

The list could continue, but, concerning Septimus, Clarissa certainly does understand why he killed himself. She is as aware of the reason for his death as she is that the Bradshaws use the suicide as an *excuse* for being late. Septimus and Clarissa are linked at last. The suicide unnerves Clarissa at first, just as Peter Walsh earlier startled her. Death is an intruder but Clarissa conceals her anxiety well; she has a true lady's discipline. No one, unless it be Peter, would guess at the tumult of emotion that blazes beneath Clarissa's pale, thin exterior. Clarissa understands that Septimus kept his "soul" through death, the ultimate weapon against Fate. Clarissa has preserved herself, her soul, in Richard Dalloway's house and within a social milieu that does not condone violence either in life or death. She prepares her days of living, just as she is trying to prepare for death. She considers consequences, lives carefully—thus is awed, and not a little envious of Peter Walsh, who has flung himself at life, and of Septimus Smith, who has flung himself at death.

CHARACTER ANALYSES

CLARISSA DALLOWAY

Clarissa has just recovered from an illness and is still frail. Her husband tries to protect her, urging her to follow doctors' orders, but then Richard has always tried to protect his wife. Despite the fact that she enjoys giving parties, Clarissa is basically shy, and Richard is also shy; therefore each is considerate and thoughtfully protective of the other. There are verbal and emotional boundaries Clarissa does not cross and there are just such boundaries that Richard does not cross. He thinks that

Clarissa's preoccupation with her parites is foolish but he never tells her outright; she is aware of his attitude because of what he doesn't say. Likewise, Clarissa is unconcerned about Richard's interests in governmental affairs; he knows about her feelings but neither one of them verbalizes what they know about each other. They do their best not to hurt one another.

There is strength in the love between Richard and Clarissa, but the strength is not made up of years of toughened scar tissue. The love between Richard and Clarissa has no scars. It is strong because both have tended it and have not torn it with slashes of anger, then repaired it with re-doubled affection. The love between Clarissa and Richard is literally that: *between* them. It binds them, loosely, but it is also a barrier — self-imposed and, for each of their sakes, protective.

Richard would like a life in the country, with dogs, but he is not able to demand it for himself. A country life is a lost dream; he is happier and more secure in his governmental post, living with his gentle, well-bred wife. Like her husband, Clarissa also has a lost dream: she would like to be able to live as fully as she realizes Peter Walsh does. But long ago Clarissa, according to what she knew about herself, realized that she would never be able to join Peter in his adventure in living. Their values were too different. Peter wanted to share himself and all that he experienced. Clarissa believed that she would never be able to —nor would Peter be able to— break away all of the fears she had about men and women and life, set herself free, and be happy. Clarissa valued her "soul" too much to give it to Peter. She was afraid of surrendering to Peter, or to life, and accepting "the heat of the sun" and "winter's furious rages." She shied away from the *way* Peter loved life. She married Richard Dalloway so that she could love life in her own intense, but inward, fashion.

In her own way, Clarissa does respond to living. *Mrs. Dalloway* contains many examples of Clarissa's response to life. She enjoys flowers deeply, inhaling their delicate sweetness and their rich earthy odors; the air rushes over her skin and she thrills to its wave-like sensations; the jangling noise of cars and street vendors stir within her. She is sensitive to the "moment," to the "poetry of existence" in all its sensual dimensions—but the excitement goes only to Clarissa's own boundaries. Unlike Peter, she is not driven to share experiences; unless Peter can "share" a moment, its value is not wholly consummated. In this sense, Clarissa is still virginal.

SEPTIMUS WARREN SMITH

Septimus Warren Smith is the other side of the coin in this study of sanity and insanity. Septimus went to war, he tried to defend his country, and he attempted to become a "man." He lost. Clarissa did not do battle; she withdrew and married a safe man who would not dare her to be more of a woman than she believed herself capable of being. And she lost. She believed that marriage would destroy both herself and Peter. She considered consequences; Septimus did not.

When the novel begins, both Clarissa and Septimus are out and about in London. Both absorb the exquisite beauty, but Clarissa does not weep at what she sees and hears and feels. She does not release and exude her excitement. Her reactions and Septimus' are similar but Septimus' are far more intense.

Both Septimus and Clarissa feel that they are outside, looking on, and at the same time dashing headlong through life. They are both alternately very happy, then very worried and fearful. Virginia Woolf shows us the moment of terror in Septimus' heart and then relates it to what supremely matters to Clarissa. To her, what supremely matters is what one "feels"—and what terrifies Septimus is that he cannot "feel." Yet despite their similarities, Clarissa and Septimus *do* differ. Septimus is concerned that he cannot feel and care for another person; he is horrified that he is unable to feel as, say, Peter Walsh might feel. Clarissa is afraid of "feeling too completely." Clarissa is a bit guilty of Sir William Bradshaw's sin—of giving service to Proportion. But, one might ask, what is one to do if he, like Clarissa, is convinced that he is not capable of flinging himself at life — and surviving? Should he make himself a willing victim? Clarissa is unlike Peter and Sally and Septimus; she does not have their abandon nor their flair for rebellion.

The quality most central to Clarissa and Septimus is their insistence on no one's having power over them. Septimus refuses to let Bradshaw use him for experimentation and Clarissa is equally as defiant of Miss Kilman's determination to dominate her. But Clarissa has also refused Richard's, and Peter's, intimacy because of her intense fear of domination. In this novel Virginia Woolf includes flaws and impurities in her major characters so that human nature, and not metaphors, are revealed.

REVIEW QUESTIONS

1. What is an interior monologue? Describe, using a specific character in *Mrs. Dalloway* and show how the monologue functions as a narrative and expository device.

2. While Virginia Woolf was writing this novel, she referred to it as *The Hours*. She changed the title, but what evidence is there of her concern with time?

3. The charge has been frequently made that "nothing happens" in Virginia Woolf's novels. How would you answer this?

4. What facets of the English social system does Virginia Woolf criticize?

5. Why does Peter Walsh object to Hugh Whitbread?

6. Describe Miss Kilman in terms of her religious feelings.

7. How, and through what characters, does Virginia Woolf weave the theme of possessiveness and possessive love?

58

8. In what way are Peter Walsh and Sally Seton similar? Peter and Clarissa?

9. Describe instances in which a "sane" character thinks or utters a phrase that is amplified in Septimus Smith's madness.

10. From the brief scene Virginia Woolf presents, describe Clarissa and Richard's marriage.

11. What are Clarissa Dalloway's values?

BIBLIOGRAPHY

Books

BENNETT, JOAN. *Virginia Woolf: Her Art as a Novelist*. Cambridge: Cambridge University, 1945.

BLACKSTONE, BERNARD. *Virginia Woolf*. New York: Harcourt, Brace, 1949.

BREWSTER, DOROTHY. *Virginia Woolf*. London: Allen and Unwin Ltd., 1963.

CHAMBERS, R. L. *The Novels of Virginia Woolf*. Edinburgh: Oliver and Boyd, 1947.

DAICHES, DAVID. *Virginia Woolf*. Norfolk, Conn.: New Directions, 1942.

FORSTER, E. M. *Virginia Woolf*. Cambridge: Cambridge University Press, 1942.

HAFLEY, JAMES. *The Glass Roof*. Berkeley: University of California Press, 1954.

NATHAN, MONIQUE. *Virginia Woolf*. New York: Grove Press, Inc., 1961.

PIPPETT, AILEEN. *The Moth and the Star: A Biography of Virginia Woolf.* Boston: Little, Brown and Co., 1955.

WOOLF, LEONARD. *Sowing: An Autobiography of the Years 1880 to 1904.* London: Hogarth Press, 1960.

———. *Growing: An Autobiography of the Years 1904 to 1911.* London: Hogarth Press, 1961.

———. *Beginning Again: An Autobiography of the Years 1911 to 1918.* London: Hogarth Press, 1964.

Articles

BOWEN, ELIZABETH. "The Achievement of Virginia Woolf," *New York Times Book Review,* June 26, 1949, pp. 1-21.

FORSTER, E. M. "The Art of Virginia Woolf," *Atlantic,* 170, September, 1942, pp. 82-90.

HARTLEY, LODWICK. "Of Time and Mrs. Woolf," *Sewanee Review,* 47, April-June, 1939.

ISHERWOOD, CHRISTOPHER. "Virginia Woolf," *Decision,* May, 1941.

SCHORER, MARK. "The Chronicle of Doubt." *Virginia Quarterly Review,* 18, Spring, 1942, pp. 200-15.

NOTES

CPSIA information can be obtained at www.ICGtesting.com
Printed in the USA
LVOW06s1119290714

396557LV00001B/35/P